Presented to

Kaleigh

From

Mike & Krista

Date

Easter 2007

the Toddler's ABC Bible STORYBOOK

The Toddler's ABC Bible Storybook
Text copyright © 2007 by Carolyn Larsen
Illustrations copyright © 2007 by Caron Turk
Published by Crossway Books
        a publishing ministry of
        Good News Publishers
        1300 Crescent Street
        Wheaton, Illinois 60187

Cover design: Caron Turk
Cover illustration: Caron Turk
First printing 2007
Printed in Singapore

Library of Congress Cataloging-in-Publication Data
Larsen, Carolyn, 1950-
  The toddler's ABC Bible storybook / Carolyn Larsen ; Illustrations by Caron Turk.
    p. cm.
  ISBN-13: 978-1-58134-802-6 (hc : alk. paper)
  ISBN-10: 1-58134-802-9 (hc : alk. paper)
 1. Bible stories, English. I. Turk, Caron. II. Title.
  BS551.3.L376 2007
  220.9'505--dc22
                        2006020211
CIP

IM 15 14 13 12 11 10 09 08 07
15 14 13 12 11 10 9 8 7 6 5 4 3 2 1

the Toddler's ABC Bible STORYBOOK

Carolyn Larsen & Illustrations by Caron Turk

CROSSWAY BOOKS • WHEATON, ILLINOIS

A PUBLISHING MINISTRY OF GOOD NEWS PUBLISHERS

is for Ark

Noah's big boat.

God told Noah to build a big boat. It was called an ark. God sent lots of animals to go inside the ark. Noah's family went in the ark, too. Then there was a big flood on the earth. Noah's family was safe inside the ark. The animals were safe inside the ark, too.

is for Baby

Baby Jesus was born in Bethlehem.

Mary and Joseph were in Bethlehem. But they could not find a hotel room. So they stayed in a stable, a place where animals were kept. Baby Jesus was born there. Mary laid him down to sleep on some hay. The animals were all around.

is for Creation

God made everything.

God made the world. He made the sun, moon, and stars. God made trees, flowers, and grass. Then he made animals, birds, and fish. God made people, too! He made everything in six days. On the seventh day he rested.

is for David

David fought a giant.

When David was a boy, he fought a giant soldier named Goliath. Goliath had a sword and a shield to fight with. David had only a slingshot and some stones. David shot a stone. It hit the giant in the head, and he fell to the ground. God helped David win!

is for Egypt

God's people were slaves in Egypt.

The Jews were God's people. They were slaves in Egypt. They had to work very hard. God wanted the Jews to be free. He sent Moses to lead them out of Egypt. God did many miracles to help the people escape from the king of Egypt and his army.

is for Fish

Some people had a fish-and-bread picnic.

Many people came to hear Jesus teach. When dinnertime came, the people were hungry. There was no place to get food. A young boy gave Jesus his lunch. It was five loaves of bread and two fish. Jesus did a miracle with that little lunch! He gave food to all the people. Five thousand people had plenty to eat, and there were leftovers!

is for Garden

Eden was the most beautiful place on earth.

God made a beautiful place for Adam and Eve to live. It was called the Garden of Eden. It had beautiful flowers and trees. It had rivers and lakes. Everything Adam and Eve needed was in the garden.

is for Hannah

Hannah prayed for a child.

Hannah wanted to have a baby. She prayed and prayed for God to give her a child. When she had a baby boy, she named him Samuel. Hannah was very thankful to God. She took Samuel to live in God's house, the place where the Jews worshiped God. There he could learn to serve God.

is for Isaiah

He was a prophet.

A prophet tells things that are going to happen in the future. Isaiah lived a long time before Jesus was born. He wrote one of the books that is in the Old Testament. He wrote about Jesus being born in the future. God told Isaiah what to write. Everything happened just as Isaiah said it would.

Isaiah 2:2
In the last days Jerusalem and the Temple of the Lord will become the world's greatest attraction, and people from many lands will flow there to worship the Lord.

is for Jesus

Jesus is God's Son.

An angel came to see Mary. "You will have a baby boy," the angel said. "You will name him Jesus. He will be God's Son." The angel was right. Mary had a baby boy. She named him Jesus, just as the angel had told her to do.

is for King

David was a king.

When David was just a boy, God chose him to be king of Israel. David fought a giant and won. He served King Saul. David loved and obeyed God. When he grew up, he was crowned king of Israel.

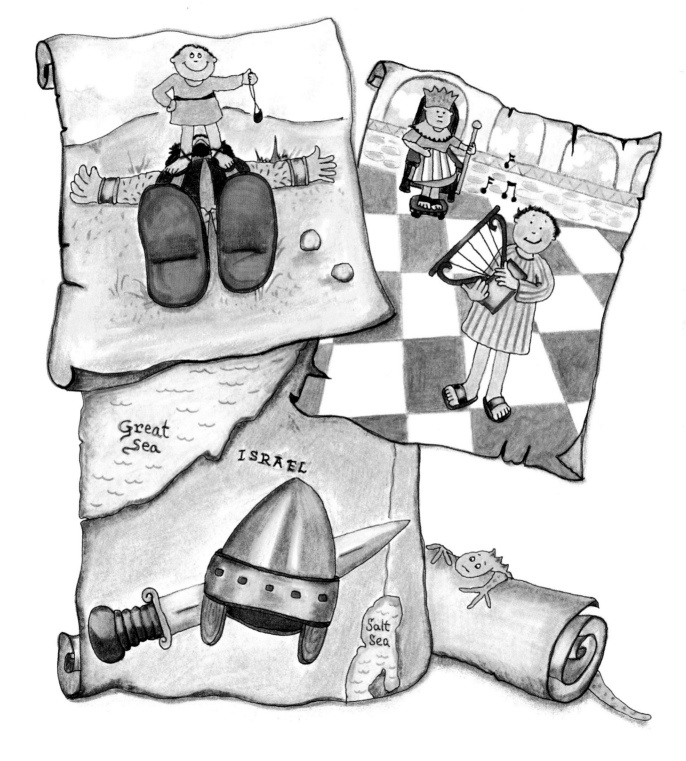

is for Lazarus

Lazarus was Jesus's friend.

Mary, Martha, and Lazarus were Jesus's friends. One day Lazarus got sick, and he died. Mary and Martha sent for Jesus. He was sad that Lazarus had died. Then Jesus did something wonderful, something no one else could do. He made Lazarus alive again! Mary and Martha were very happy!

is for Moses

God gave Moses a special message.

Moses was the leader of God's people. God told him how to lead the people. God called Moses to come up a mountain. He wanted to talk to Moses alone. God gave Moses special rules for how people should live. They are called the Ten Commandments. God wrote the rules on a piece of rock for Moses to take back to the people.

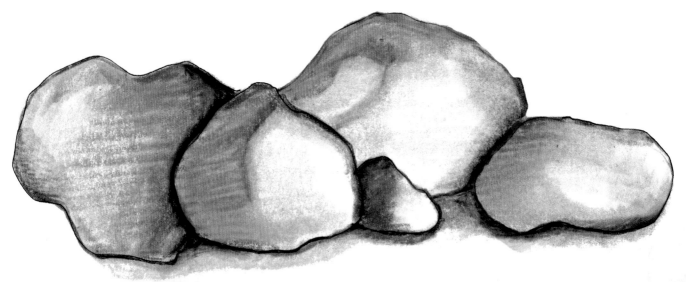

 is for Nazareth

Jesus grew up in Nazareth.

Nazareth was just a little town. It was not important or famous. But Mary and Joseph were from there. After Jesus was born in Bethlehem, they moved back to Nazareth. Jesus grew up in that little town.

is for Oil

A woman had all the oil she could use.

A woman owed a man a lot of money. All she had was a little oil. She asked the prophet Elisha for help. Elisha knew God would help her. The prophet told her to start pouring her oil into jars. God did not let the oil run out until all her jars were full. Then she sold the oil and paid the man all she owed.

EMPTY

is for Paul

Paul taught many people about Jesus's love.

Paul did not like people who loved Jesus. He was mean to them. He even put them in jail. Then one day a bright light from heaven shone in Paul's eyes. He heard a voice asking why he was hurting Jesus's friends. Paul knew that the voice belonged to Jesus. He was so frightened he fell down on the ground. Right then Paul began loving Jesus, too. He spent the rest of his life teaching others about Jesus.

is for Queen

Esther was a beautiful queen.

A king had a contest to find a new queen. Many beautiful girls came. Esther was the most beautiful of all. She was also very kind and wise. The king chose her to be queen. A bad man wanted to hurt the Jews, God's people. He didn't know that Esther was Jewish. She asked the king to help. He got rid of the bad man, and then the Jews were safe! Esther was also very brave. When she and her people were in danger, she risked her life to get help. Today the Jews remember her courage on a special day each year.

We love Queen Esther

is for Rainbow

A rainbow showed God's promise to Noah.

A big flood was coming. It would cover the whole earth. God wanted Noah to be safe. He told Noah to build a big boat. God sent animals to go inside the boat. Noah's family went inside, too. When the flood was over, God put a rainbow in the sky. It showed God's promise that a flood that big would never happen again.

is for Samuel

Samuel heard God speak.

Samuel was just a little boy. He lived in the Lord's house and helped the man in charge there. This man was called a priest. One night Samuel heard someone call his name. He ran to see what the priest wanted. But it wasn't the priest who had called. It was God! God had a special message for Samuel.

is for Ten

Jesus healed ten men.

Ten men had a very bad disease. They could not live with their families. They had to live in a special place away from healthy people. The men asked Jesus to help them. He did! Jesus made them all well. But only one man remembered to thank Jesus.

FAR AWAY

is for Uz

Job lived in the land of Uz.

Job had seven sons and three daughters. He owned lots of land and animals. He was very rich. Job always tried to obey and honor God. But then Satan tried to get Job to turn against God by taking away all of Job's money. He did terrible things to Job. But Job did not turn against God. He loved God very much. In the end God gave Job back everything he had lost and more.

MONEY

ANIMALS

Sons

DAUGHTERS

LAND

is for Vegetables

Daniel ate vegetables.

Daniel was being trained to work for the king. He was served special food. It was very good. But Daniel didn't want that food. God had given his people certain rules about food. Eating the king's food would break those rules. Daniel wanted to obey God. He asked for only vegetables to eat and water to drink. At the end of the training, he was stronger than all the other boys!

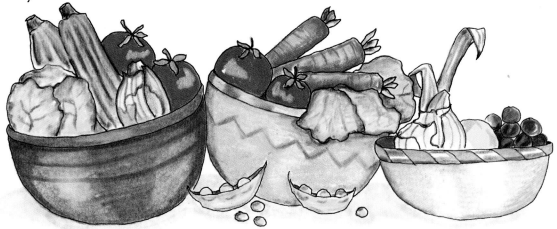

is for Walls

There were walls around the city of Jericho.

God told Joshua to capture Jericho. But there were big walls around the city. "March your army around the city once a day for six days," God said. "On the seventh day march around it seven times. Then shout, and the walls will fall down." Joshua obeyed. The walls fell down, and he captured the city.

is for Xerxes

Xerxes was a powerful king.

King Xerxes chose Esther to be his queen. He loved her very much. Esther told him that a bad man wanted to hurt her and all her people. King Xerxes stopped the bad man. He saved Esther and all the Jewish people.

To Esther

King Xerxes

Y is for You

Jesus loves you.

Did you know that Jesus loves you very much? The Bible teaches that God sent his Son, Jesus, because he loves the whole world. That means you!

is for Zacchaeus

He climbed a tree to see Jesus.

Zacchaeus was not a nice man. But when he heard that Jesus was coming to town, he wanted to see him. Zacchaeus was too short to see over the crowd. So he climbed up into a tree. Jesus saw him in the tree. "Come down," Jesus called. Jesus went to Zacchaeus's house for dinner. After that Zacchaeus was nice to everyone.